CRYING ON MY BIRTHDAY

by Holly Way

Dedicated to myself,

for all the times

I was stronger than my frailest parts.

FOREWORD

Every week, I attend a writing group in Melbourne. It takes almost two hours to get there and just as long to get home, but it's worth it to get away from my desk, talk to other writers and get creative in a different environment.

One particular night – the third of August, less than two weeks ago as I write this – I really had to force myself to go. The weather was unforgiving, pouring and freezing cold. But I had been unproductive all day, and I knew that I usually get more done in my two hours at the group than in a whole day at home, so I put on as many clothes as I could find and forewent bringing my laptop along as it would have surely been drowned. Instead I grabbed a pen and an exercise book and went on my way.

I'm telling you this because this was a serendipitous beginning. If I hadn't shoved myself out the door and into the icy rain that night, you wouldn't be holding this book in your hands. It was that night that I wrote a poem intended to explore the symbolism of trampolines in my adolescence and ended up with a heart-wrenching (to *my* heart) recollection of my fifteenth birthday. That's the thing about writers: what we think we're writing is rarely what ends up being read.

Line after line, draft after draft, poems write themselves until they have become what they were always supposed to be. This one transformed into something that could not stand alone, that begged for companions. I couldn't say no. I didn't want to.

Sharing is – like most things worth doing – terrifying. What if no one gets it? What if I'm just not talented? What if I put in all the work and nothing happens?

In contemplation of these questions, I came to a realisation: art, I truly feel, is not a request to be understood, nor seen, nor celebrated. Art is merely the *product* of the artist's endeavour to understand *themselves*. A detective's messy whiteboard, connecting this thing to that. To make art that is meaningful, we must embrace the ink stains and let go of our desire to make art that is – for lack of a better term – "good." Expression which is self-conscious is not truly expression at all. Humans require vulnerability in order to connect.

So I set out to understand myself. More specifically, I wanted to poke the dead body that is my habit of crying on my birthday every year without fail. And having poked it so aggressively in such a short window of time (extracting many more tears in the process), I haven't yet had time to digest all the lessons this book has to teach me.

I can't say I don't feel different. I relived the past ten years of my life, and none of them were too pretty. I put myself under enormous pressure with my determination to publish on my upcoming birthday (because I'm a ridiculous, poetic idiot who likes the symmetry), giving me three weeks and one day to get my shit together. It wasn't only the deadline, but the financial and logistical strain of self-publishing, ensuring I made good on my other professional commitments and battling the poorest mental health I've had in years all at the same time. I could have cracked under the weight of it all. Instead, I grew stronger.

These stories have been lurking in my mind for a decade, and as frightening as it is, I'm glad they are finally seeing the light of day.

Are they good? Who knows!

What matters is that they've been written.

Thirteen

Suburbia-cheap,

please-take-a-seat,

all-you-can-eat,

not a soul here for me; a dozen

fluorescent pubescents made up in a rush

and eyes down so as not to blush

and trying not to eat too much

and phones under the table

til my mother says *enough*.

French fries and

French onion soup and

piles of frigid

unripe fruit (it wasn't ready

to be plucked from the tree just yet –

should've waited til the skin was red.)

And the cake

comes in a box

that I keep for memories –

cards from Woolworths written

by all the boys' mothers,

and the pictures I take

with my two-year-old brother,

and the way I just know

that I'm not like the others,

for the ritual song,

for the loud mouths moving,

for the soft serve melting by the heat

of my salty young tongue

does not tell me

that it matters

I was born,

does not tell me

what matters

at all.

Fourteen

I'm known

to treat attendance

like a deadly disease,

but squeeze

the pus out of it

and it isn't so bad,

a sprawling six hours

spent traipsing

through the grass, dampened

by dew spittle

licking our shoes – sorry excuses

for protection from the rain.

Metal tongs and plastic buckets,

chasing after rubbish

'til it's very soon enough

and we instead sit talking

by the bricks against the gym,

losing breath for silent laughter.

This feels

like something

'til the lunch bell brings the flood.

Crowds are hollow shells,

all the insects on the outside,

snaking,

crawling,

licking up the crumbs before

I know someone's been eating.

Home is not hollow

but pregnant

with a sense of

duty

both hostile and resigned,

so that candles are ignited

but their smoke is a roared *goodnight*.

Cuts require attention

so the in-betweens are lost;

those spaces that lull,

schoolyard like a ghost town,

the comfort in the silence

and the innocence of touch

cannot compete

with a cannibalised brain,

snatching scoldings just to plant them,

bound to blossom

in the overactive greenhouse

of an adolescent mind.

Fifteen

In six months

he's morphed

from willing devotee

to dog on a leash –

pull it tight

so I've got something to rage against.

I worship a man

who wants to fuck a fourteen-year-old

and gets credit for his patience;

what a saint

to settle for handjobs

for all the nights

of the foreseeable future.

I worship a man

who steals my sanity on a daily basis,

and I don't ask questions

like *should I struggle against*

these hands

round my butchered neck?

or

how can I love a person

who treats me like a rash?

I worship a man

who sends a text on my birthday

I'm gonna see a movie with dad instead,

and I think that's love

and I beg him to reconsider

and I think *that's* love

and I am

so fucking honoured

to be served a slice

of his precious mirthless time.

See

I get what I want

but it comes with a catch,

disaster homing swiftly on our methylated breath,

Jim on the fire

to engulf the black of night –

watch where you step;

glass travels like water

and your feet are young and naked,

take it for granted

that the wave takes nothing from us,

leave the fire burning

while we follow the bending bitumen to the yellow

    lighthouse sanctuary of Mooroolbark McDonald's.

I join my fellows' protests,

begging for fries through the window of this aromatic

    oasis

despite insistence by the night staff

that the restaurant is closed.

This interaction, it seems, is a punishable offense,

a betrayal of trust,

the act of a whore,

for my honey's off running,

scathing sentiments

tumbling backways as he goes,

flying past my wheezing body

while I push on after him

quick as I can,

quick as I can't,

no room for tripping

in the dance *de l'amour*, I'm learning,

taught again,

when I slip in the rancid darkness

and fall on fragile knee,

haphazard chasm forged deep in my alabaster skin.

His phone rings unanswered,

unbothered,

no caution for the girl he left

chasing

chastised

through a school under construction

in the middle of the night.

And he waits 'til I find him,

dozed off back home

aglow in the warmth of the fire,

to tell me that he's leaving,

and I'll swallow that motorbike whole

before I let him climb on it

with his words soaked in stench

of so many raspberry vodkas –

do anything,

and that's the point; forgiveness by default

in case your curses are final words.

The low rumble ceases

and my body sighs its sighs,

and it's time for bed

but we don't go there,

not realising how cruel it is to sleep

where in summer

where in dazes

where fragrant grass and barely knowing

too hot to touch

lips only brushing,

where eaten alive by morning and woken by the sun

a man and a minor

so quickly fell in love

(or something like it,

or something not).

But that was January

when the weather made us sweat;

August has us flinching,

mouths meeting roughly in obligatory amends,

those red-stained lips,

his threadbare hips,

static on the trampoline

and bruises on my ribs.

And my moans are for my sorrow

and the pressure on my knee,

and is this what it's all about?

I am exhausted

by the way that he loves me.

Sixteen

Queensland took my kin from me,

entrapped them with its balm,

warm showers in the winter,

humid breath

rising from the pavement

leaving me

lonely sentinel

preserver of my life,

clinging to my reasons

as their fingers unfurl their grasp

on my pink and slickened hands.

In the bedroom –

once a study –

of my aunt's tidy townhouse

I have never felt more crowded

yet so crushingly alone,

independently dependent,

paying for my heartbeat,

last two dollars

go to a dinner of Homebrand potato chips.

And whether it's atonement

for last year's mishaps

or the past few months of

unrelenting isolation,

nobody knows,

but he for whom I left my roots planted

shows up in the morning

with good spirits I no longer recognise

and an offer to make me breakfast.

Somehow

I end up cooking

as he makes it known

he has the whole day off for me,

and my cheeks hurt from smiling

so much

so early

so out of practice.

The thing is I had plans,

grown up twisted,

accustomed,

entwined around the lattice of my unwanted solitude.

So he comes along,

takes my hand,

kisses me in public,

bodies trembling

through the shudder of the train.

Today

I am eligible for an allowance

and there's no time to spare,

so we spend the day

in the Dehumanisation Department,

speaking low about nothing

while the girl across the way

thinks about stealing my runners.

I feel like a common beggar

not deserving of a scrap,

and I've grown up with empty pockets

but it's different when yours

are the only ones to feed you,

and your friends all live at home

and you feel already grown

and growing

out of everything.

And this hand in mine is

an illusion,

and I should know that

but I don't; not until

the green sticks in the clock read 12:01am

and it's all over

and I'm alone again

knowing

that all love is August sunlight,

at mercy to the clouds –

how dangerous to bask in that fleeting warmth

believing

it will last forever.

Seventeen

I'm looking for some speakers

that'll deafen us

tonight

when my mum's home fills with people

who have nothing else to do.

Just this once

I tell a stranger it's my birthday,

price drops,

too steep,

price drops,

too steep

(but I buy it anyway).

In everything that matters

there is always music

and if I can get it whistling high enough

I'll know

that I'm of import.

Chasing that rhythm costs me

savings worth a whole week of wages,

washing hair for a living

but still

can't afford to live.

I make it

out of the cramped and downlit salon

just in time to change my face

before the guests arrive

with well wishes,

arms full of liquor,

I drink

whatever I can get my hands on.

I drink enough

to forget how vacant my stomach,

and then enough

to forget how tight my clothes, how

lately the hips

defy all starvation,

round, wide and waiting,

waiting on and on and on.

I drink enough

to forget that this party is for me,

and call a taxi to take me elsewhere

with the boy I want to kiss

(and some more

I wish I could've made stay

back there where I found them).

Four delinquents traipsing

up a quiet rain-oiled street,

my street,

Slevin Street, where the homes are owned

and the owners old

and the property value went crashing

when they crammed community housing in that block

    on twenty-four.

My eyes

keep on opening

to a new texture underfoot,

memory sewn together,

a tattered quilt of image and assumption

joined to one another

by the feeblest of threads,

and I'm that teenage trainwreck

my neighbours want me to be,

a fixed vessel for their resentment,

fumbling for my key

at the door to my temporary living space

which contains my bed

and my dread

and all my things,

but cannot be called a home

by a human statistic.

Swing open,

down mattress,

hair snipped

floating,

falling,

resting on the bathroom tile.

Hot water,

skin scalding,

house full of boys

writing cards on stolen Styrofoam;

Free Canna Lilies,

no touching,

night bleeds through the sunrise,

missed chances, walls between us,

hair in shades of chocolate

woven into the carpet,

living in the fabric

once its owner leaves for good.

Eighteen

Vodka is my drink of choice;

watch it drown me as I beg for salvation.

This is what I get

for demanding a fuss.

The girl I've grown tall

in my rose garden

douses my weekend in

fluid from her lighter

and sparks from her match.

But nobody blames her –

not even me –

we spend our love on roses

and forgive them all their thorns,

eyeballs undulating, film surface set in waves,

I lay the blame inwards

where it probably belongs,

for what gall I had

extracting a weekend from a year

and telling it how to treat me,

two weeks of milky tea

and barley sugars melting

ginger spices on the tongue,

always morning

no matter how many times I brush my teeth.

And all to wake up eighteen

with my claws still in my stomach,

so ensnared by the lure of perfection

I won't ever be enough,

dry skin and cold marrow,

black spots on open eyes,

size twelve is for monsters and I'm edging on fourteen.

I always take my vodka straight

like a toddler taking medicine,

paint stripper sliding

down a semi-swallowed throat,

cure me of my cowardice.

What are friends for?

They know to keep on pouring

when I say I've had enough,

and they haul

my heavyempty body

from the toilet to the bedroom,

no flicker,

no sirens,

serenade my corpse at midnight

with a haunting rendition

of a hymn called *Happy Birthday*.

Bed so wet with sweat

I think I've pissed myself on my first day as an adult,

and if I had any sense

I'd abandon my perfect weekend

for fluids and rest,

but my brain's all scar tissue,

core coding set to *strive*.

So I let myself be woken at nine

and shoved in a shower,

walls made of seaweed,

kaleidoscope recollections stirring sickness in my

    waning cage of flesh.

I'm still not certain

this day was not promised to death.

I scrape my insides for a shred of gratitude

just like the Vegemite

scraped from its jar and then

scraped onto toast,

try eating it,

so dry that it chokes me,

but I've a sister and a friend

with whom to attempt

to actualise my fantastic production

of a day of congratulation,

sophistication,

drinks with lunch,

only now I can't stomach it –

the train ride I sleep through

and the sea in my stomach

and the call from my mother *I won't make it there in time.*

The day passes quickly

with no hint of want for life,

get it over with, running late to dinner,

slow train and fast makeup

and I arrive just in time

to spend an hour switching tables

so they all had a reason to show.

I treat the restaurant bathroom

like a walk-in robe,

change of clothes

as if I am leading

some sort of double life,

and if I am it's the world's worst kind,

hiding scars in my stand-up,

fists clenched making half-moons

just waiting for a chance to end it.

I haven't worked in two months

but I've got two outfits

and a stretch Hummer limo

and a hotel room waiting

on Little Collins Street,

solutions to my throbbing problems,

I promise – just you wait and see.

Ringwood to Melbourne,

people shouting,

neon leaking,

I don't feel real,

I don't feel *here*,

we hang out of the windows

screaming *love me,*

love me now,

bring me honour,

bring me down,

tap my veins,

bleed me out.

Eighteen and

free and

here so early,

witness

to the silence in the music,

spaces stretching

like maternity pants round a swollen belly,

sparse pockets pulsing,

all the same as us;

suburban hoodlums looking for big life elsewhere,

too restless to stay home,

too cheap to miss the pre-ten discount.

My net expands and cracks open,

new clubs,

new addictions,

new phone, new affliction,

no answers,

no calls,

I spend the night holding up the line,

locked in cubicles

forsaking my mascara as I carve

obscenities into my putrid reddened flesh.

The girl beside my body

in the sullied hotel bed

finds sleep without effort

while the telly plays *Cheers* 'til morning

and my thighs are torn to nothing

and I'm rueing all my wasted money

and I'm wasting all my ruined years

and I'm beginning to think

that's just the way it is.

Nineteen

I give myself permission

to eat this weekend.

As if I have the authority.

What that means is

a long stretch of unshakable hunger,

blood slower,

bone-deep,

earning interest in advance

on those weeks of self-denial,

and when it's over

tremulous mouthfuls,

purple hands grasping,

greedy;

just one more bite.

Half an hour scouring

the menu, all vegan, I can eat anything

here, overwhelmed

with choices – how will I punish myself

tonight?

Narrow it down

by finding the largest

and most greasy of meals

and calling it mine

with a pizza on the side –

when you have leftovers

you have a reason to eat tomorrow.

I dine with Guilt nightly

on meals of tea and water.

The more I feed her,

the bigger she gets,

a tomb door boulder in the pit of my rotten stomach,

who doesn't leave

even when the food does.

I pass the night

with a jar of toothpicks set loose in my abdomen,

bent double like a thick book closing,

no days off

from this rabid infection.

You can't have your cake

if you're going to eat it.

T w e n t y

Soft vanilla cupcakes,

icing plastic-blue –

my sister made them special while I spent the day at

   school.

She even bought me a book

about sustainable fashion, and I guess

I've done a good job convincing everybody

that after two years

choking

on the fumes of my self-destruction

I am very much okay;

eating and learning and laughing and leaving the house.

Nobody knows I'm dropping out again,

quitting something else

because I just can't stand it,

can't finish,

can't start,

can't rise up in the morning

just to prove I haven't died yet,

because my brain works like it shouldn't

and tells me that it should

only put its efforts into

fire and ice

and leave the lukewarm for the others

who don't need to walk the fringes

just to keep themselves sane.

Making clothes feels like

a toe dipped in a pool,

and when I'm singing

I am engulfed in the ocean

and thinking of nothing at all,

and that's what I need –

I need to be drowning

so I know that I'm alive.

And maybe if I worked the other way,

chasing after dollars

instead of after feelings

I wouldn't be where I am –

moving in with my mother

so we can both afford a roof.

I would be working for a living

supporting us both,

giving mum some time off

from her role as matriarch

of a poor and failing family.

But I don't have any candles

to make that wish come true,

so I eat a blue cupcake

and thank my sister for the book.

I really mean it.

Twenty – One

I long to be the kind of child I never was,

lost in joy's sensation

and not its dry pursuit.

I wake up so determined to be happy

that I cannot really feel it

and so determined to celebrate

it reminds me to ask *what for?*

Twenty-one years ago

I was born – and so what?

It makes more sense to celebrate

the time I wrote a suicide note

and didn't kill myself –

chose to open my eyes tomorrow,

and tomorrow

and tomorrow.

What if

twenty-one years have all gone wasted,

better spent on someone typical

who can wake up on their birthday

without knowing they will cry?

And what if

it's narcissistic

to demand a form of worship

one day

each year

'til I finally up and die?

And then,

when I'm dead

to demand a deeper mourning

one day

each year

'til the day *you* up and die?

And what is

attention

and why do we seek it?

And who am I

in the lens of a camera?

or a pane of reflection?

lost in translation,

lost in translation.

The person I am

when nobody is looking

is the person I want to be.

But what if

it's my fault,

like I forgot to add something to the recipe

or to take something out

once I got older.

After all,

though not carefree,

I was a child once,

who kept all her cards

and smiled through the song

and blew out the candles

with a wish

tingling in her fingertips,

delicious

but forbidden

from putting in her mouth to speak it.

I was a child once,

who believed in backyard fairies

and the colour of the sky,

and awaited August twenty-five

with the patience of a dog

awaiting their walk.

And was it

that anticipation

that spoiled it

or my own spoiled agenda?

That voice of mine that tells me

the grand moments should be bigger…

Deep down

I just know it – that

this day is not for me,

for someone with a heart so bitter

and so full of wonder,

and so broken,

and so immune to satisfaction

it can never be at peace.

Twenty – Two

I have friends again

for the first time in years

and it does not even occur to me

to inform them

that today I am another year older.

Is that proof of my indifference

to this annual tradition

that has caused me so much pain,

or merely an expression

of my textbook modest tendencies,

unwilling to ask for

unwanted,

unwarranted attention?

It seems like such a strangely-strung sentence,

informing people of your birth date,

a demand within itself.

It's only in the dome of family

that I feel obligated to mark the day,

an urge

that is no more than two decades of habit.

My sister, in a devastating burst of famous good
    intentions,

condemns me to a day of purgatory,

barred from the kitchen,

lonesome wanderer homebound

and clueless with no end in sight.

I walk with my brothers in the pre-spring afternoon,

and there's an apathetic silence

drowning out the songbirds

looming overhead

like the threat of a death ward pillow.

Every thought I voice

sounds petulant,

horrendous when said aloud.

No less grating inside my head.

Back home

I am punched in the gut

by the efforts of my sister –

a day's work in edible,

and I wish it would open up

and swallow my ungratefulness

and my deep wells of self-importance

and allow me to smile so much larger

and validate the trying

so it feels like it's enough.

This day

is the lie

that I can't stop believing,

that can only hurt me

if I do.

Palms,

fists and then relaxing,

flexing in and out.

One day

I'll keep them open,

outstretched and accepting

whatever may come or go.

Twenty – Three

If all goes to plan

the first eyes reading this

are doing so

on the very day

that I am twenty-three years old.

On this day

it is my promise to myself

that I will try my very hardest to be happy –

not because

I have made it round the sun again,

or because there is something

inherently special

about the twenty-fifth of August,

but because

it is a day

that I am alive

and breathing

and a unique glued-up smattering of ancient space
    debris wrapped up in

human casing,

human goodness,

human flaws and neuroticisms,

so different

and so very the same,

alone

and a part of something,

violent and beautiful,

vital and irrelevant,

perennial and irreparable,

and if I deserve to be celebrated

I will celebrate myself,

devote my life to it

so that every time I am older

I am better in equal measure,

and if I indulge

in a little melancholy

or great disastrous grief

on any day of the year

that is not

some crime of feeling,

but my right

to let the lows flow through me

so they might at last flow out.

I do not claim to be content

or safe or balanced.

I cannot say for certain

that no tears will come today,

for life is frustrating

and to let go of the hope

that one day might stand outside of it

is to break a cyclic burden

that has known me all my life.

Dearest reader,

with my book held in your hands,

you have seen the billowing flags

planted in the milestones of my strangest, darkest
  years,

one day a culmination

of the three hundred and sixty-five before it,

an invitation to ask for all the things you want

but do not have.

Perhaps if I had been taught it differently –

a day not for seeking what you lack

but loving what you hold –

I would not need to leave it behind.

And I know I do need to, even if not today,

but one August

when I'm Parisian

and no one but me,

and I'll tell far and wide,

j'ai pas un anniversaire, mon ami,

and I will seek other ways

to make sure I am growing,

like the art that sprung

from toxic soil

and flourished in your hands.

ACKNOWLEDGEMENTS

Thank you to the universe (or whatever) for every human, animal and miraculous display of nature you've put in my way. There's not a single one that did not leave its mark on me, and consequently on this book.

Thank you to my mental illness. My sensitive soul. My maddening empathy. Thank you for the rough road that forced my feet to grow calloused so I could walk through terrain that many could not handle. Thank you for allowing me to see the world differently.

Thank you to the few blood relatives I call family. You make me laugh, you make me cry, you make me absolutely fucking crazy. You made me keep on living when I didn't want to stay. Thank you for loving me even when I'm hard to love. I love you more, you idiots.

Thank you Rhiannon, for being my sister, my best friend and my number one fan (as I am yours). Thank you for being as fucked up as I am and for all the meandering conversations that go nowhere and mean nothing. May there be many more.

Thank you Hayley & Sarah, my first real friends and my own personal cheer squad. You give me so much strength. The world needs more people like you.

Thank you Frances for honouring my little book with your beautiful, epic artwork. I can't wait to watch you take over the world with your army of 2D babes.

Thank you to anybody who is reading this because you follow me on social media. Thank you for listening when I shout into the void. Thank you for your support, no matter how you choose to give it or how insignificant it feels to you – it means very much to me. I appreciate you.

And last but not least, thank you. You. Whoever you are. Thank you for giving my words life by reading them. I hope that they have given you something in return.

Holly Way is a writer of poetry, fiction, social commentary and anything else that takes her fancy. She lives in Melbourne, Australia, and when she isn't writing she is eating vegan food, sleeping with her cats or attempting to dismantle the patriarchy.

Crying on My Birthday is Holly's first book.

You can find more of her work here:

www.wattpad.com/wayholly

www.twitter.com/wayholly

www.wayholly.tumblr.com

www.instagram.com/wayhols

And if you want to help Holly publish more books like this, consider becoming a patron:

www.patreon.com/hollyway

Cover design by Frances Cannon

www.francescannonart.com

cannon.frances@gmail.com

www.ingramcontent.com/pod-product-compliance
Lightning Source LLC
Chambersburg PA
CBHW032049290426
44110CB00012B/1017